Heart First into the Forest

Heart First into the Forest

Stacy Gnall

Alice James Books
FARMINGTON, MAINE
www.alicejamesbooks.org

10 9 8 7 6 5 4 3 2 1

Alice James Books are published by Alice James Poetry Cooperative, Inc.,
an affiliate of the University of Maine at Farmington.

ALICE JAMES BOOKS
238 MAIN STREET
FARMINGTON, ME 04938

www.alicejamesbooks.org

Library of Congress Cataloging-in-Publication Data
Gnall, Stacy, 1983-
  Heart first into the forest / Stacy Gnall.
    p. cm.
  ISBN 978-1-882295-87-6
  I. Title.

  PS3607.N345H43 2011
  811'.6--dc22

                              2010044568

Alice James Books gratefully acknowledges support from individual donors, private
foundations, the University of Maine at Farmington and the National Endowment for
the Arts. ❦

Image of Alice James by permission of the Houghton Library, Harvard University.
Call number: pf MS Am 1094, Box 3 (44d)

Cover art:
Eugene Grasset, "Three Women and Three Wolves"
Musee des Arts Decoratifs, Paris
Bridgeman Art Library

Table of Contents

Acknowledgments

Gratitude is given to the editors of the journals in which the following poems first appeared.

The Cincinnati Review: "Self-portrait as Thousandfurs"
The Florida Review: "Ars Perspectiva" and "The Insecticide in Him"
The Gettysburg Review: "Primal Elegy"
Indiana Review: "Ode to Superstition" and "Trespass"
The Laurel Review: "Halloween, Ohio, and an Appropriately Named Lake"
Prairie Schooner: "Damsel, Stage Directions," "From a Dance Manual," "Singing the Cannonball to Sleep," and "What the Child Was Given Next"
Spoon River Poetry Review: "The Funambulist"

With admiration and affection, I'd like to thank all the teachers who have ever encouraged me in doing this thing I love—especially Thomas Lux for telling me I had "the disease" and Jeffrey McDaniel, to whom I owe more than I can say.

Thank you also to David Welch, Jeremy Hawkins, and Ryan Browne—indispensable editors and friends—as well as to anyone else who has had even the slightest hand in helping me with these poems, or who has shown me even the slightest love.

To everyone at Alice James Books: I thank you for your support and kindness, and for taking a chance on me in the first place.

But most of all, I thank my best friend Nick Parker, my brother Steve Gnall, and my parents Gail and Stephen Gnall. This book is for you.

Damsel, Stage Directions

She must wake
in a place she doesn't recognize—

bound, surrounded by debris
of other lives—find her way out.

She must have broken
away from the group—

naive as the number one,
naive as she is half-naked

and barefoot now—running
with a limp (injury implied),

a bruise slung mink-wise
about her neck.

She must fall just once in the chase
over bramble, antler, root—

the scene around her
dizzy, a revolving door—

stupefied by the setting
sun and the birds

in on it too, throwing
their voices, trying to confuse.

She must glance always
over her shoulder,

gasping to lose him,
to outsmart the lunatic

trees, her face unfurnished,
a puddle with nothing

to reflect—glancing—
the fish rolling back in her eyes'

blank lakes—glance—the moon
a fat, white mosquito bite

itching her on to where
she ends at an edge of road,

spots a truck's grill
wavering lazy in the horizon's heat,

laughing a little,
coughing up berry-worths of blood

and muttering what she can
only muster, sputtering into the cement,

into the dense, senseless
air of summer: I made it.

Ode to Superstition

You come on
strong
as sun
in the middle of day,
a grueling matinée—
as imaginary,
as thin
and with consequence
as the equator.
If x,
then a lifetime
of y.
If not
heads up,
a hex.
What strange
hand-me-downs,
superstitions—
awry heirlooms
swallowing
societies whole,
leaving little
breathers
tied to tethers.
What color
on four legs
crossed
our path?
How many magpie?

Enter the house
with the right foot
and leave
without sneezing.
You dome
of vain hopes,
throat
with a dirge
built right in,
slow elegy
for sense—
take the soul
that escapes
with a yawn,
have October's
immunity
to opals.
Another
frenzied bride
backward lobbing
her bouquet.
If, then.
Logic slain
like a maiden
name.

From a Dance Manual

for my father

> *Treat me nice*
> *Treat me good*
> *Treat me like you really should*
> *'Cause I'm not made of wood*
> *And I don't have a wooden heart*
>
> —ELVIS PRESLEY

Snip the cranky thing from its crib.
Rest its potato-scented head against your lapel

and carry its teacup weight, the world's
youngest antique in your arms.

Then permit the rug your promenade.
Follow imagined dance-map feet.

Behandel sie gut.

Sing, scavenger of the lowest notes.
Make your way through the German verse,

that bit of violence in the back of your throat.
Behandel sie gut, behandel sie gut.

On TV, the second shuttle's success.
Outside, the ambient logic of snow.
You've lost your job. You dance.

Past the mantel's burden, past each bashful knick-knack.
Hum, and she will grow to be gruff enough.

Past the blue-gray glances from the photographs.
Bellow, and she will be burr fierce. Coo.

Past the wreath, the hearth, the paisleys in their frenzy
on the ironing board, sway.

And she will chase ghosts and wolves away.
Twist, and men will treat her well. Whirl.

Past the patience of the piebald hobbyhorse,
treat her good, treat her good.

Sing, and the thing will fossilize.
Dance, and it will petrify.
Her heart will be a beating bit of bark.

Behandel sie gut.
Treat her good, and it will turn into wood.

What the Child Was Given Next

This is the thanks she gets.
The dark. And the unknown

goings-on as the eye adjusts.
Her foundling fright on all fours.

This is what she gets.
For trusting the beastly embezzler,

for having the sweetest ingredient amid the trees:
what's soft and tropical under a frock.

This is what.
To sit in his breadbox,

a stone, a callow Jonah,
now solemn as if going to school.

She is thinking of her sampler.
She is whiling away the hours,

sees each stitch in the line
from scripture, the stomach now

skeins of skin, brocade.
She is reciting the names of days.

She is walking heart first into the forest.

That every one may receive the things done
in his body according to that he hath done.

Yes, this. But what thanks
that when the hunter comes,

though both red,
the heart will come after the head.

That when the hunter comes
to slit the snarl from where it wells,

this will be she: from the bowels
a rouge bowl to be dipped and dipped from.

In the Basement of the Late Tussaud

There is a place

on the skin's palette

for this:

what the sense

of touch expects,

but is given instead.

The slash, the brand, the blow.

The message sent

through the cells

as in a water brigade,

'til the world narrows down.

Lost in the red lace of the brain.

There is a place

on the skin's palette

for this:

the slash,

the brand, the blow.

In the basement

of the late Tussaud,

the message sent

through barred cells

by death's brigade.

On the pallet,

an entourage of implements.

A tawdry show

and tell. What meat

from the market

stolen, what gossip

spoken. Leaving scars,

the loved ones of the blade.

What pageantry pain.

There is a place.

In the basement

of the sculptress Marie,

an eternal inquisition,

accusations in orbit.

The slash, the brand,

the blow.

Perennial attempts

to blackmail the body.

Believing that underneath

their nails, below

the masks' bolts, swirling

in the eclipses of hoods,

they have secrets.

And on their palates,

answers held

captive

by wax.

Trespass

for my mother

Once

    when you could still smell the green on me

back when your looking old was new

we ran to the dark churchyard
        and under God's empty bell.

The dimmed silver held us in its huddle.

Its walls refused
    the lawn's stichic hieroglyphics.

It was colder than moon.

Together we pushed its great weight up

      but nothing.

Its round rim could only mouth *mother*
      to the night.

A lark then.
    An absent cloud.

The bell with its tonsil out.

    The three of us unable to make a sound.

Pantoum Before the Killer Comes

Nothing at stake in their landscape,

just feet from his father's wrecker,

stripped straight of restraint on the vista,

they wide-eye their way toward each other.

Just steps from his father's wrecker,

she's soft in the yellow clover.

Wide-eyeing her way toward her lover,

ready and open as a right answer.

Hand down in the golden clover,

he marvels at her minutiae.

Open and ready as a right answer.

She plants a small death on his neck.

Hand marveling her minutiae,

her torso trills below him.

On her neck, he plants a red death.

Her body bends in oath beneath the oak.

Her torso thrills below him,

their reflection severed in the wheel rim.

She bends her oath beneath the oak.

The girl breathes in, the boy breathes out.

Their reflection severed in the wheel rim,
the sun high as a front-page headline.
The girl breathes out, the boy breaths in,
light as the sigh before a storm.

The sun bright as a front-page headline,
it will read *In the light of day...*
Light as their sighs before the storm.
In their landscape, nothing at stake.

The Insecticide in Him

Leaning against the stubborn shed, my brother looks right
and sinister with his shirt untucked.

He is a hopscotch-skip away,
speculating what a second tongue tastes like, the contents
of a schoolgirl's skirt, about babies: how one plus one makes three.

He clacks his gum, his tongue a pin in a pink balloon.

With a start, he pulls a firefly from the marmalade jar,
a pulse of magic and flint blaring Sunday! Sunday! Sunday! on his knuckle.

In this light, he looks more like an x-ray of a boy.

He stares square into the insect glow, twists its wings and tosses them back
into the air, snaps his fist closed and holds its half-beam body to my nose
so I can see: its insides are a contortionist's kiss, the sorry smell of blood and iron.

He says *witches live in their guts*.

He is always teaching me these things, like how the business
section makes the best-floating boats, and some stars even wear belts.
How when the man comes home to the wife, he fits perfectly inside.

Bella in the Wych Elm

There were no marks of disease or violence on the body,
but her mouth had been stuffed with taffeta.

—BRIAN HAUGHTON

She through the rootlets.
She murked by moss.
She in its whelm.

She the owl in the tree
trunk's mouth stretched
to canvas a scream.

She the taffeta still
in her teeth.

She slight in the night's dark
peignoir, eyes on the sky
so long stars disappear.

She flesh left
for the air to edit.
She year after year.

First, she gold rush of hair
as she collapse, light
avalanche from the hands
that ferried her there.

She slung on his arm
and set—an epaulet.

She first dragged
down the woods' brusque
tangent, first taken
from the tousled ground.

She a splurge—scarved
and sexed. She slim consent.
She the throat's spangled
cackle and choke.

She first in the trysted park.
She in his arms his lips the grass.
Through the rootlets.
Murked by moss.
In its whelm.

She our sleep
thrashed and thrummed.

She spurns our nerves,
she trips our veins.
She missing reel,
we scratch the blanks.

She for his mantel.
She for your mantel.
She my trinket too.

Self-portrait as Thousandfurs

To have been age enough.
To have been leg enough.
Been enough bold. Said no.
Been a girl grown into that
negative construction. Or said yes
on condition of a dress. To be yours
if my skirts skimmed the floors.
To have demanded each seam
celestial, appealed for planetary pleats.
      And when you saw the sun a sequin,
the moon a button shaped from glass,
and in the stars a pattern
for a dress, when the commission
proved too minute, and the frocks
hung before me like hosts,
to have stood then at the edge
of the wood, heard a hound's bark
and my heart hark in return.
      To have seen asylum in the scruffs
of neck—mink, lynx, ocelot, fox,
Kodiak, ermine, wolf—felt a claw
curve over my sorrow then. Said yes
on condition of a dress. To be yours
if my skirts skimmed the floors.
To have demanded each seam
just short of breathing, my mouth
a-beg for bestial pleats.
      And when you saw tails as tassels,
underskins sateen, and in entrails
damasks of flowers and fruit,
when the bet proved not too broad

for you, and before me, the cloak held
open as a boast, to have slipped
into that primitive skin. To have
turned my *how how* into a howl. To have
picked up my heavy hem and run.

Ars Perspectiva

Taking the long way home and thinking of the dead,
on a two-faced day, torch-bright but bitter, I walked
in the middle of the road and the road through me,
when a ribbon of deer, outright and easy, spooled ahead,
the biggest—the obvious heartthrob—leading the way.

The trees—deer—silently swayed, playing charades,
sending their little memoirs to the ground—deer.
Underground, bones in beautiful wardrobes,
I thought, and still: deer—deer—deer.

The sound of feet meeting ladder, and suddenly aware
I was not alone, a man, paintbrush in hand,
looked down from a house to the ribbon then me,
the look between us a tender trophy.
Big family, he struggled to say, in an English
poured first through a sieve. Or was it just wind?
Big family, big family.

Nights, when dreams threaten
not to look both ways before crossing,
I think of him, telling our chapter
at market, over dinner, in front of the fire.
Sure is, the girl said then, he tells his sons.
Sure is, sure is.

What Gets Me Today, Frank

to O'Hara

What gets me today, frank
world, is the multitude.

The many momentaries.
And the momentum passed

from transient you—confident
as a continent—who moved through

the mongers and the motives,
half man and half morale.

Today, from your blocks,
wafts a big band bouquet.

Subway bison, chorus girl clicks,
the low round growl of the moon.

All the slipped names
lift where you left them.

Denby, Bonnard, Koch, and Joe.
Pennsylvania Station.

Lillian, Fanny, Sonia, Jane—
all your starlets in the sky.

Your hum-colored
cab's sweet snag on me.

This—a radiator clank, a cap gun banner's
BANG—gets me today, Frank.

That though it was all obligato
(this you had in common with the cannibal),

for all your bounds and bountiful,
you always knew how to find the tender

center of the city, the pulse
in the pocket—your Reverdy.

This gets me, this sways,
this really hooks-jabs me

today and, with it, the agony
of your casual, your feigned traipse.

That despite the show of hands,
your lines were more preen than plash.

That since you spoke so plain to us,
we—your hidden track—come

to you like a cross street,
think we can talk that way back.

Halloween, Ohio, and an Appropriately Named Lake

This is how we do water in the Midwest.
The waves. Their sound is not as much
a round of applause as it is a golfer's clap.
You're narcissistic. You and your ocean.
You and the sun with your initials scrawled across.
But I think you look good too, so on Halloween
I'll dress as a hand-held mirror for you.

See, I've reserved Lake Erie for us,
and as we push away in our canoe, our eyes
touch everything, and it turns to costume.
The sky is a negative of a ghost, a black sheet
with star-slits for eyes, the lighthouse a hero
flashing *his* x-ray eye, and the flagpole on the shore
is the world's tallest matador waving, *Ole! Ole! Ole!*

Forgive me. I'm from a state shaped like a heart,
and this thought raises my soul as though by séance:
the seaweed bending in our direction, extending a dance,
the undead eyes of infinite fish surrounding us. And me,
setting aside my oar, bobbing for your Adam's apple,
whispering, *See what a haunted house my arms make.*
Then like a bully child: *I dare you. Spend one night inside.*

Singing the Cannonball to Sleep

At night, he sleeps with his mouth just open
   and his helmet fastened tight.

See how he hugs his knees—
   harm hibernating in his hands there,
always prepared to give the ready sign.

With the light slipped into something more
   comfortable, the dark now pulled
up to our chins, and our children's things

on the carpet—the paddle ball, the army man,
   the duck you must pull with a string—
those leftovers from a day of ravenous play

all watch as he talks from within a dream:
   something about hopelessness, heftlessness,
taking to the top—the man-made sky of the tent.

Sleep is his most difficult stunt,
   but each time since our first time,
this is how I lull him: I tilt back, fill my mouth

with pine needles, clay, a copper coin.
   And when we kiss, I slip my tethers in,
say, *Rest your perilous head,* and for the first time

that day he can finally feel some weight,
   gravity's good fortune no longer eluding him,
his two felled feet no longer neglecting the ground.

Uninventing the Wheel

after George Ferris

He must have been a bicycle in a past life,
his ambition driven like a spoke.
And unsatisfied that we were awed only once
by a wheel. So he set to reinvent bewilderment.

> *You and I once loved only at certain*
> *altitudes—fire escapes, hot air balloons,*
> *and on the Ferris wheel a marriage proposal.*

If I could go to the edge of that century,
I would find him, divert him, change
the subject. Slip a sweep of whiskey in
his tea, so he'd nod off before his epiphany.

> *Words that made my ears pop.*
> *I could see the future from the top,*
> *eyes casting lines and catching the sun,*
> *a coy vanishing point on the horizon.*

His idea for its hulking grace. Before
he could ever lift lovers, oblivious voyeurs,
their hearts beating a waltz as the wheel
bragged its way through the day.

> *Now, I can't look. I drive past fairs*
> *and stare ahead, tisk-tisking my periphery,*
> *the sly persuasion of the mind*
> *thinking things away into thin air.*

That wild-eyed man with wheels in his head,
that architect of pleasure, never alive at all,
and this century's best napkin sketch never sent
spinning, the O of each mouth never uprising.

> *I'm parked outside the fairground gate.*
> *One by one, the carts in their orbit vanish.*
> *The lines of waiting people disappear.*
> *The whir of the wheel in air, the breeze,*
> *gone—along with you—asking me to stay*
> *suspended together forever.*

The Lace-keeper's Lament

Just as well that this be my lot.
To tend such a finely-knit flock.

Days, I make their velvet cribs,
their canopies of glass.

Nights, I call them home,
calm their open rustling.

What man could want my needle eye,
my neck always bent to the web?

What man could win my spinneret
having had bedfellows so rich, so delicate?

Goodnight, Shoplifter

for D.W.

> *The Romans had stolen the silkworms*
> *from under the very noses of the Chinese.*
> —WORLD BOOK ENCYCLOPEDIA, 1952

Imagine the monk mid-smuggle—
his task spun roughly before him.

Beneath the scrutiny of the stars,
past the stirring in the goblet trees

and beside the river bent at the waist,
he rests for the profanely lit hours

in a cave—its acoustics amplifying
desire, disaster, the lack of a gap between.

O, my want-eyed, tucked, my aberrant
hand—the hand the patron saint of take—

what Justinian itch makes you thief? What
just mother couldn't make him take them back?

Hush. Imagine the monk's clutched slumber.
In his hands, a fat green secret to be spooled.

Dissociative

now without pounce   you tell me   when in back of the house   looking

to flee to the trees   lining chimney   and close to the bush   where the hutch was kept

you were frightened   again in the old house   you are frightened   the rabbit   is gone

mother saying weeks   it's been months gone   and when your mouth moves away

from the moment   the wired distance   softening   your daunted state   states away

I wonder what more you're missing   from that place   with pink brick dimmed   by

what   you don't remember   what else you might as well   or worse   have never held

The Hypochondriac's Canvas

after Poe

> *For me at least…there arose out of the pure abstractions*
> *which the hypochondriac contrived to throw upon his canvas,*
> *an intensity of intolerable awe, no shadow of which felt I ever yet…*
> —"THE FALL OF THE HOUSE OF USHER"

Toward the ponderous jaws of the frame
his flashing forth   his brush   its quiet violence
his arabesque   *(But if it weren't for the legs)*

From feeble gleam to wild light   his eye
(Not quite what it used to be)   in electric sympathy
compassions shadow   encoffins color   toward gemmary

To and fro   the paint falls promiscuous—
an arresting avalanche   a bowl irreparably broken
a satellite burst   and the pesty breath of its fumes

(Damn the click of the hip)   he moves   he's double-winded
his bugaboo   his head   *(always the deep temple ache)*
is a narrow home   its sense   the rattling of a sash—

One thought   pressed and pressing   an oppressive flower
open   as an insect wing   pinned to point out the structure
bold   as a dog nailed up   *(mind the shoulder)*—its inappropriate splendor

From pillar to post   he pigments   'til in a half-swoon   with a stroke
simple as to round off a sentence   a stroke as to signature a bank note
he steps aside   (and for once forgets his arms)   to reveal
a single square of color   an enthusiastic epistle   of sickly chartreuse

The Bee's Recurring Dream

When he wakes to his brother's hum,

sleep still heavy on his wings,

and the wind through the keyhole of the hive

hints at something sweet,

he tries to shake a feeling.

All bees are petty thieves and their mother's boys,

mischievous scouts sent to drink up their badges.

And the floozy flowers are indiscriminate.

They open themselves to anything with wings.

But today, when he's surrounded

by a harem of flowers, he hesitates.

As he moves from pink to purpler massacre,

he is a dash of nerves.

Even as he's drawn home to the other drones

and joins them, mad in their geometric labs,

he thinks: *What if?*

What if the first, as it flirted in the grass

at Adam's knee, fought off the urge—

the pull to that first generous pistil?

What if the first taste set no flush-hot,

opulent fever burning in his head? What then?

Then would we know only bitterness?

Then what would he build? What would grow? What

would be waiting in each dark heart of the honeycomb?

Then We Dropped Our Hands, and Without a Word, Ran to Catch up with the Rest

We accepted the cave's invitation,
and for the first time knew regret.

Our stomachs dropped with the thermometer,
and we were suddenly on leave from life,
as hypotheticals reflected in our eyes:

From above, anvils. Stairs that never touched ground.
Below, bottom halves of totem poles
stretched toward the highest painted face.

The tour guide took us through the nether,
sure to point out earth's accidental sculptures:
rocks shaped like lions' heads, temple spires,
a map of the five Great Lakes.

Sure, too, to give us a chemistry lesson:
our hands held spoiling oils,
and if we touched the stone,
it wouldn't grow for three hundred years.

She moved toward a gash where a man
is said to have wept for years, but we
held back, feigned interest in another erosion.

Something in the rubble had turned us.
One typewriter tap, one fingerprint of impact
was all. But it would be ours.

The metronome of the dripstone paused
for a measure. Each echo held its breath.
All the hanging formations bent
their heads to say grace.

We looked to each other, fingers poised,
the dare darkening the pupils of our eyes.

Above us, places, people, and their playthings
spun like a mobile at a million tilts per minute.
But we were motionless: two
brash-faced figurines cut from the crags.

We blinked. The earth around us
suddenly so enormous.

Elemental Missives

To Water

Think back to your first cell—
to your schools of blind eyes searching

through this barnacle, that urchin,
the slim choreography of seaweed,

for something more. An armada
of modest molecules. Minute,

discontented treasure chests
ready to burst through the surface.

Think back before bone, hair, before aha,
before what god or gull come to swoop us up,

come to save us from simplicity.
Before we fell out of love with floating,

rose up from the muck of your lagoon, mouths
watering, our fathers all forgetting how to swim.

※

To Fire

What did your father do to you?
And did your mother in her hairpins turn away?

In the mirror, you see a master plan.
You will set your bright-hot branches howling.
You say memoirs, scarves, and scarecrows will be sorry.

One plume, two. You spread your red rumor
through the room. You spread your bejeweled vengeance.

In photos you are always dead center, a rash rising
through the roof of the house. It's not your fault.

Livid light, where are you going?
And who in your babbling hands will you take with you?
What sphere do you hope to reach?

You are an irrational dance, a boy in love with nothing
but himself. I light a match and watch your ego grow.

To Air

We have had enough of your heartache,
how you wake in no one's arms,
but slip through the sieves they make.
Whine, wind, whine.

Cry yourself to sleep.

You bachelor, you fleeting thing—

breezily loving then leaving

the lungs. How often have we

begged you, bartered with you, gasped

and grasped for you? And how many times

have you turned your back, or with no hand

holding no knife, stabbed

us in ours? You ugly virtue,

you lovely, lovely vice.

To Earth

Dirt, can we begin
with forgiveness?

It's taken so long to write.

But soil, we are senseless
half-sisters. Estranged
because we're so alike.

Our hearts marked
by hoofprints.

Our skin crumbling
under claws.

Bones eroding
within us, dust: a slow,
long southern drawl.

In this, ground, grant me
your contrary trait—

your strength
without complaint.

But first let me
plant, earth. Let me
bend low and trace my name.

Red-handed in the Fire's Rise

If an adult were guilty of such a sin,
one remedy was to declare the child a witch.
—PATRICK CARNES

What's sweet catches flame more swiftly.
What's secret, too. The breath withheld stokes the coal.

A man's hand on the wrist as to hands tied to a pyre—
sex sanctum and sex savage: all the same.

Your last words spoken in sleep.
Upheaved and led knock-kneed
to the commons. Quiet, but for

the match flash and its static
riding your throat like a radio.
A flue from foot to trite sky.

To say the smoke's still suspended there,
refusing to release your shape: untrue.

By the time you took the stand, you were already ash.
There's nothing, round world, warm girls, that I can do.

Lost Child in Forgotten Tale

And of a sudden here I am
saying suddenly.   Suddenly
the world went white. Moot.

And though lonesome is best
left unsaid,   I was.
Though nothing had left me.

But what a something that
suddenly   it wasn't
there. Had never been.

And though I hadn't known
I'd wanted it,   suddenly
I'd have held my breath

for that ember. That pinch-
sized life.   Breadcrumb
from a basket. Tip of a bird's

beak that suddenly speaks. Please.
Take this walking   flaw.
Awed by it as we have always been:

the body so perfect, so im-.
And it's   suddenly
so simple. It's like this:

never under the mob-cap
clouds will I be   a mother.
Never into the green wide wood.

Take me 'til it suddenly
doesn't double   me over.
'Til it only dips me like a frond.

A Brief History of Being Burned to the Ground

The rules of the reconstruction were rigid:
must haul twice your height in flame, your ashen weight
written in the ledger left-hand-wise, wretched.

It was the spring she came across a starling, unsewn.
Its insides so much slender—blue coils, electric—
and this before electricity in the village was known.

Her mouth brushed open by those wings then, an O,
the shape disbelief takes, and her blue voice said,
Bless it, bless it. Its bones. Žehnáj to. Žehnáj to.

And Mirek's mind by then his butcher's block.
Thick and riddled red as calligraphy ink, his threats
to heave from high, drop, and slice. Just watch.

And her mother by then turned to water, a water slick,
a cascade in her apron dancing, always the drafty
dancing, startling everything still intact with a kiss.

She danced to the soft shapes disbelief makes,
pressed her *Baba* lips blue. She danced to the shape
of Emelia, vague mother of the Byzantine saint.

But with the missing shapes of scaffolds and trestles,
slants of shutters and cusps of beams, to her it was clear:
the dance, the body, the ankle—all superfluous angles.

Every step then a cliff, a risk, and twice their size.
The story in each new warp of wood, of a city between
its buildings, between its build and rebuilding.

Accidental Outlaw

Already, mother, I can sometimes see
a memory hanging like a hammock
in your head—swinging between those
trees etched *remember* and *forget*.

One day, a game of cowboys
who have lost their Indians. You
will grab at your past, the names
of neighbors, and my face
with a threadbare lariat, driving me
farther and farther away. My
words tumbling like a weed through
your mind's abandoned corral,

swaying back and forth like saloon doors.
You will be confused, but still
beautiful, holding a dishrag
like a sheriff's badge in your hand.

And of all the things I've ever
hoped for in your one-horse life,
this is all I will ask when you die:
that when your soul, that bandito,
steals away, all the surrendered memories
will line up like cavalry. You will
mount them, set in the direction of God
knows where, and ride.

Or Iron Heinrich

after "The Frog Prince or Iron Heinrich" by the Brothers Grimm

Late-arriving Heinrich, soldered servant,
with your heart a knuckle wrapped in brass—
          your name belies the title.
Spell-annulling night sheds its vestments. Sun enamors the East.
And you report with ostrich-plumed palominos.
          You guide their cold bits. You ride.
                    Everything gilt-leaved but the trees.
The carriage is falling apart—
risers and rails clang, unfettered. Spring bars and bows clap their strain.
But it's not the conveyance
that makes this cadence. It's you that swerves and skews,
          Heinrich, as the foundry falls from your chest.
                    As the foundry falls from your chest, Heinrich,
just this once: let the clamor last
          another clause, let it rattle for one more passage.
Let the *once again and yet once again*
the cracking be pattern for a chapter.
Let the weight of the king's missing slip from your withers,
          and bray at your freight slow and long.
As when the master leaves and comes home to the dog, Heinrich.
The beast breaks in two then into song.

Unquieted Calvary

The dead are tired of lounging around—hands folded
        across hearts, pledging
                allegiance to cedar.

The stones on their graves are fixed flags,
                    surname-spangled
        banners marking each small empire of earth.

In Calvary Cemetery in Queens,
        these flags are raised to full mast.

The sweat of one's brow is what burns.
                The dead grow restless.
    The Irish have said this.
                And they have started pushing.

They are pushing against the bases
        of the slabs that class them,

pushing out through the smug, brown
            soil surrounding them.

They are pushing to recall
        the sweet weight of work on the shoulder,

the elbow's compromise,
          the fingertip's fine appliance.

They are pushing to feel the wingspan
                of effort spread
                                in their chests—

        the stones exhaling for them.

The Funambulist

Name: Girolamo Zini
Occupation: Rope-walker
Location: Istria/Trieste
Cause of Death: Atlantoaxial Dislocation
—THE MÜTTER MUSEUM, PHILADELPHIA

You live in a disease museum, a physician's vaudeville,
home to cold diagrams and graphs, those attempts
to map the tubes and sewage inside us.

Among immodest organs and muscle
demanding attention, stares a wall of skulls,
all hung like death's dumb trophies.

Below the brain case of a boy who was once
a shoemaker's apprentice, and beside the embroiderer of silk,
your skull waits patiently for its next life, Girolamo.

You do not wire-walk to the sound of the calliope.
You do not shake the hand of gravity.
Your skull just sits, a vase once filled with breath.

This is what you see as you climb the ladder:
The women who peer up through the pinholes of hands,
the men who pretend they are solid as Roman numerals.

You glance to the children you will frighten by simply walking away.
Then you will move across the taut rope towards safety,
sequins, the girl on the platform with the impossible waist.

Is this what it is to exist, Girolamo? To touch toe to rope
for a moment, to test how thin of a world we can stretch
our weight over, only to fall when our skin has broken in?

Here, where students of the ache learn to listen
to the *blub blub* of that badge we wear behind our chests,
learn to drag our insides like lakes for evidence of infection.

Yes, now Girolamo, as the security guard is turning away,
let me blow into your bare nostrils and make them flare,
paint the color back in your face as though by number.

Girolamo, I will pull the red breath from your mouth
like a magician's scarf. I will tiptoe you to safety.

Flare

Wait.

> Through trees
> with bursting limbs,
>> I am running.

Blending with bark,
> a mute blaze.

My eye's blue stain
> on the green

I am running
> toward the stream.

Past names scratched,
> last summer's lean-

to, the ravine bridged
> by a held breath

I am running
> toward the game.

Toward the arm.

> The birds cutthroat
> in the clearing I am
>> running toward

the twist. Running
> toward the same as

away. Toward the twist-
> arm game by the stream.

My eye's blue, running.
> Under canopy, I'm nothing.

Feet between deer tracks,
> I'm vanishing. A burst,

held breath, and over
> anthill, say grace.

Wait.
        Bright flash,
    big brother, I am
            catching up to you.

L'échapper Belle

How the world loves the sleight of hand—
trees pulled endlessly from the earth's black hat,

the sun keeping the colors of leaves up its sleeve,
and even the little girl now by the door

of the Houdini museum, exchanging a dollar with *her* slight hand.
Her eyes are two wide tickets as she steps inside.

What question marks will be around these corners?
The dull knife-light along the carpet leads

to a display on the pranks that mirrors pull, a collage of locks
scuffed from struggle—the brawls between his own two fists.

A reel projects stunts: the threat of rope, straitjackets, burlap sacks.
He is suspended from a crane over the Atlantic.

The sights turn the white scarf of her face into a fluttering dove,
slice her and leave the saw inside.

Until now, the only magic she'd seen is bread rise, eggs hatch,
grass that grows between cracks in her street.

But alchemy was his everyday—the finale,
from flat-top to spats, his life-sized statue

she walks past—*Ladies and gentlemen*—and catches
a flash. Did he just—*and for my next trick*—move?

Oh! That little horror from the corner of her mouth
as he steps from the stage, his cards fanned out

in a blunt bouquet: *Pick a flower, any flower.*
A diamond dances from the deck. A club crashes out of air.

Was this—a heart fades into a spade—*your card?*
—that suit, its dark Valentine shape.

She's missed him by so many years, she thinks.
And yet, he has illusioned this escape:

as she moves through the exit and squints
at the bright of the street, she feels herself

part down the center like a red velvet curtain,
and all that had been hidden behind, steps outside.

Primal Elegy

—God's last animal
lost in the first forest.

Where now that dash, that cower?
Again day ends. Again

dawn spreads its orange encore around.
Time with its muzzle and bridle.

We tame: a book folds over the boldest word.
Our brute is only breath on the cold.

But once in a great white while
the prim fog parts for the slight primals.

There in the light by which boys bully.
Whiskey's burn and scurry.

And in the violet, skyward tonight,
the sound of a lover fast unwrapping his sweet.

Smothering the Howl

The worst beast has broken from the totem.
Locks spring open at his approach.

Was it mercury caused his mercilessness?
Or having thirsted from footprints?

An epileptic then, born the seventh son squared,
Or from yellow marsh a lycanthropic flower dared?

The worst beast has broken from the totem.
Locks spring open at his approach.

Name him: shape-shifter, skin-walker, unwed
Warrior, pelt from the head of Berserker.

Name him for his bravado: *Rogue.*
For his fickle cloak: *Turncoat.*

Warg: for the slight realist chance
It's a madman's cyclic attack.

Name him for where your mother's from:
Hombre Lobo, Lupo Mannaro, Rougarou,

And for the fear he'll there find you.
Or just name him for what will be left: limb

In a field. The worst beast has broken from the totem.
Locks spring open at his approach. You must know:

To remove his shape, his shadow, to the hewn tree go.
Kneel there for one hundred years.

Say: *Come silver's stream, Come amulet eyes,*
Come drool of the dog drugged by honeycake.

Say: *Elf, zwölf,* come death of the wolf.
Softly fan him as he lies.

NOTES

The italicized lines from "What the Child Was Given Next" are from 2 Corinthians 5:10.

The epigraph for "Bella in the Wych Elm" is borrowed from an article of the same title on www.brianhaughton.com.

BOOK BENEFACTORS

Alice James Books and Stacy Gnall wish to thank the following individuals, who generously contributed toward the publication of *Heart First into the Forest:*

Mary Jane Chizmar
Matthea Harvey
Andy and Mary Kosko

For more information about AJB's book benefactor program, contact us via phone or email, or visit us at www.alicejamesbooks.org to see a list of forthcoming titles.

This Strange Land, Shara McCallum
lie down too, Lesle Lewis
Panic, Laura McCullough
Milk Dress, Nicole Cooley
Parable of Hide and Seek, Chad Sweeney
Shahid Reads His Own Palm, Reginald Dwayne Betts
How to Catch a Falling Knife, Daniel Johnson
Phantom Noise, Brian Turner
Father Dirt, Mihaela Moscaliuc
Pageant, Joanna Fuhrman
The Bitter Withy, Donald Revell
Winter Tenor, Kevin Goodan
Slamming Open the Door, Kathleen Sheeder Bonanno
Rough Cradle, Betsy Sholl
Shelter, Carey Salerno
The Next Country, Idra Novey
Begin Anywhere, Frank Giampietro
The Usable Field, Jane Mead
King Baby, Lia Purpura
The Temple Gate Called Beautiful, David Kirby
Door to a Noisy Room, Peter Waldor
Beloved Idea, Ann Killough
The World in Place of Itself, Bill Rasmovicz
Equivocal, Julie Carr
A Thief of Strings, Donald Revell
Take What You Want, Henrietta Goodman
The Glass Age, Cole Swensen
The Case Against Happiness, Jean-Paul Pecqueur
Ruin, Cynthia Cruz
Forth A Raven, Christina Davis
The Pitch, Tom Thompson
Landscapes I & II, Lesle Lewis
Here, Bullet, Brian Turner
The Far Mosque, Kazim Ali

Alice James Books has been publishing poetry since 1973 and remains one of the few presses in the country that is run collectively. The cooperative selects manuscripts for publication primarily through regional and national annual competitions. Authors who win a Kinereth Gensler Award become active members of the cooperative board and participate in the editorial decisions of the press. The press, which historically has placed an emphasis on publishing women poets, was named for Alice James, sister of William and Henry, whose fine journal and gift for writing went unrecognized during her lifetime.

TYPESET AND DESIGNED BY MARY AUSTIN SPEAKER

Printed by Thomson-Shore
on 30% postconsumer recycled paper   ·
processed chlorine-free